P9-DNF-529

Communities

Contents

Judy Nayer

A Rural Community

This house is in a rural community. A rural community is in the country, and the houses are often far apart. This house has fields and farms around it.

In a rural community, some people live on farms. Others may live in the nearby towns. This is a rural town. People work in the banks, restaurants, offices, and stores here.

In a rural community, children take a bus to school. Since people live so far apart, children may have a long bus ride to school and back.

In a rural community, people may have to travel a long way to go to a supermarket. They might also buy food in the smaller stores in their community.

A Suburban Community

A suburban community is near a big city. Houses are often close together in a suburban community.

In a suburban community, some people work in office buildings like this one. Many other people have jobs in the big city nearby.

In a suburban community, some children take
the bus to school. Children may have a short
bus ride to school because the school is not far
from their homes.

In a suburban community, many people drive to supermarkets. They might buy food for a week. They also drive to shopping malls.

An Urban Community

An urban community is in a big city. It has many, many people. Some people live in apartment buildings. Others live in houses that are close together.

In an urban community, many people work in tall office buildings like these. Other people have jobs in shops, factories, restaurants, and hospitals. There are lots of jobs and lots of places to work.

In an urban community, many children walk to a school right in their neighborhood. Some children may go by car or bus to get to a school in another neighborhood.

In an urban community, people can walk to stores. There are many different kinds of stores in an urban community, and people can shop in a big supermarket or at a small store. Most urban shoppers buy what they can carry home.

Three Kinds of Communities

	Where People Live	Where People Work
Rural		
Suburban		
Urban		

How Children Get to School	Where People Shop

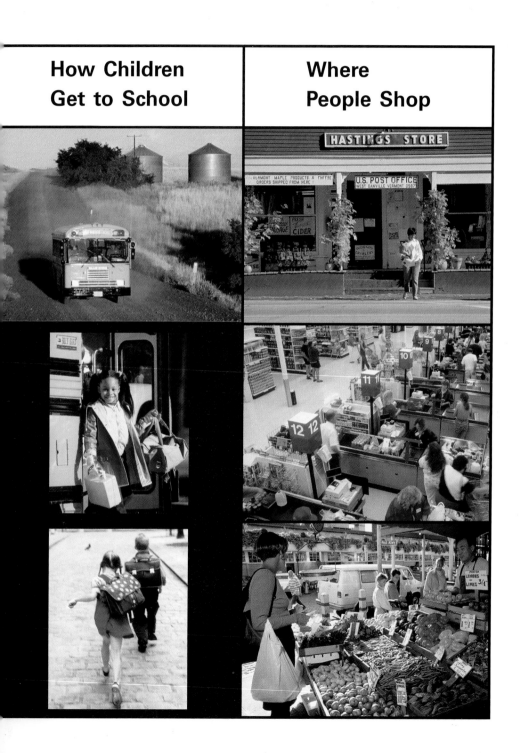

In the United States, people might live in a rural, suburban, or urban community. They work, play, go to school, have fun, and share special times together there.

Which kind of community do you live in?